IMAGES
of America

PHILADELPHIA
NAVAL SHIPYARD

*This book is dedicated to all the men and women who made
this country strong by their work at the Philadelphia Naval Shipyard.
Well done! Also, I'd like to dedicate this book to my parents,
Joe and Veronica Ahern, for all of the support and encouragement they give me.*

In 1851, the world's first floating dry dock was built at the Philadelphia Naval Shipyard.

IMAGES
of America

PHILADELPHIA
NAVAL SHIPYARD

Joseph-James Ahern

ARCADIA
PUBLISHING

Published by Arcadia Publishing
Charleston, South Carolina

Printed in the United States of America

For all general information contact Arcadia Publishing at:
Telephone 843-853-2070
Fax 843-853-0044
E-mail sales@arcadiapublishing.com
For customer service and orders:
Toll-Free 1-888-313-2665

Visit us on the Internet at www.arcadiapublishing.com

Contents

Acknowledgments

I would like to express my thanks to all those who helped in the creation of this book: Kellee Blake, Dr. Robert Plowman, and the staff of the National Archives Mid-Atlantic Branch for the opportunity to intern at the Archives, which lead to this work, and their assistance in the selection and pulling of the photographs; I would also like to extend my appreciation to Beryl Rosenstock for her valuable advice in the publication of this work, Mike Reil and the technicians at PCI Group Inc. for their great work in reproducing the photographs, William Stepler for his assistance in the identification of various photographs and his knowledge of the Yard, and the staff of the Philadelphia History Museum (The Atwater Kent), and the Camden County Library-Voorhees for their support and encouragement during the research and compilation of this work.

Introduction

Philadelphia has always been a maritime city. As the birthplace of the the nation and largest city in the young republic, it was only natural that when the United States Navy was formed in 1795 Philadelphia would play an important role in its start and growth. The first of six frigates authorized, the *United States*, was launched in 1797 from the privately owned yard of Joshua Humphreys, credited as the first Naval Constructor, near Old Swedes Church. A year later, the first government-owned yard in Philadelphia was started when two docks were built.

The official start of the Philadelphia Navy Yard came in 1801 when Congress authorized the Shipyard to occupy 10 acres along Federal Street in the Southwark section of the city. The property was valued at $37,000. For the first years of its life, the Yard handled ship repair and maintenance. With the War of 1812, Philadelphia began to accept new construction projects, the first being the 74-gun ship-of-the-line *Franklin* launched in 1815. Thirty-four more warships would follow, including the famous side-wheel steamer *Mississippi* in 1841, which served as Commodore Matthew C. Perry's flagship on his 1852 expedition to Japan; the 120-gun ship-of-the-line *Pennsylvania*, christened in 1837 before a crowd of 100,000; and the first screw-propelled ship, the *Princeton*. The Yard also built the world's first floating dry dock in 1851. The American Civil War signaled the coming of change to the Philadelphia Navy Yard. Besides an increase in employees (from 345 to 1,750) and work, the war showed the need for more ships and a larger facility.

In 1868, the Federal government bought League Island, 800 acres of land at the confluence of the Delaware and Schuylkill Rivers, from the City of Philadelphia for one dollar. With 5 miles of waterfront and room for expansion, League Island was the perfect spot for a naval shipyard. As operations were being moved, officials maintained both locations until the Southwark Yard was officially closed in 1876. During the slump years following the Civil War when the demand for shipbuilding declined, the Yard witnessed many physical improvements. These included installation of an electric light plant, roadways, concrete sidewalks, railroad connections, and a sanitation system. The first two dry docks were built in 1891 (supervised by Robert E. Perry who later discovered the North Pole) and in 1898 during the Spanish-American War.

At the beginning of the twentieth-century, work at the Shipyard consisted mainly of scrapping, modernization, and reconditioning warships. With American entry into World War I, ship construction returned to the Shipyard. The first vessel built from the keel up was the transport *Henderson* in 1917. This period also saw the installation of the 350-ton hammerhead crane at Pier 4 and the construction of the Navy's first and only propeller manufacturing facility in Building 20 (which is still operational today). After the war, work fell off at the Yard, especially after the signing of the Washington Naval Treaty in 1922.

With the start of World War II came the Yard's golden age (from 1939–1946). During this time, the Yard built fifty-three ships, and converted or overhauled 1,218 more. Civilian workers at the Yard went from 4,500 to 47,000 (excluding part-time and subcontractors), with an excess of 70,000 military and civilian personnel passing through the gates daily. In 1945, the name of the Yard was officially changed from the Philadelphia Navy Yard to the Philadelphia Naval Shipyard (PNSY). The various projects totaled more than $1.6 billion for the U.S. Navy and eight Allied nations.

After 1946, work at PNSY began to specialize in electronics and missile checkout projects, emerging in the mid-1950s as a leading facility. Yard activity fluctuated during the Korean War as Yard personnel rushed to place vessels from the reserve basin into active service. PNSY also participated in the Mutual Defense Assistance Pact program (MAP), overhauling and refitting ships for European and Latin American nations. Construction projects assigned to PNSY during the early Cold War period were few, but ranged from guided-missile frigates to amphibious assault ships. Ship construction at the Yard ended with the 1970s, by which time nearly one hundred and fifty ships, from wood sailing vessels to aircraft carriers, had been built.

From this point on, work in Philadelphia consisted of modernizing destroyers, overhauling conventional submarines, and conducting repairs on ships. The Yard's reputation for safety, efficiency, and impressive workmanship won it the Service Life Extension Program (SLEP) contract to modernize five aircraft carriers in an effort to add fifteen years to their service lives. This project brought the return of aircraft carriers to PNSY and helped rejuvenate the work force. In 1990, the U.S. Senate honored the Philadelphia Naval Shipyard as the most efficient of the Navy's eight yards. However, this was not enough to secure the future of the Yard. That same year Secretary of Defense Dick Cheney announced plans to gradually close PNSY as a result of military cutbacks.

For the next six years, shops were closed, employees were retrained, and plans were made for use of the shipyard. In 1994, the city was given control of the land, with the exception of the areas used by the Naval Surface Warfare Center, the Foundry, and the Reserve Basin (all of which remain active). After the aircraft carrier *John F. Kennedy* left Philadelphia in 1996 following modernization, the Philadelphia Naval Shipyard was officially decommissioned. When it closed, the Yard had 1,326 buildings, 52 miles of streets, five dry docks, thirty-four fixed, floating, and portal cranes, and had grown to over 1,400 acres. With its many accomplishments and ability to provide any service needed, it is no surprise that the Philadelphia Naval Shipyard was the "mainstay of the fleet."

All photographs are courtesy of the National Archive-Mid-Atlantic Region.

Joseph-James Ahern
New Jersey
April 1997

One

The Yard

When the Philadelphia Naval Shipyard moved to League Island in 1876, the U.S. Navy was in a period of decay. These Civil War-era monitors, docked at Philadelphia in 1887, were seen as the symbol of the nations maritime strength. The Yard would play an important part in rebuilding the American Navy. The building in the background is Quarters "A," which was used as a V.I.P. quarters and later as a temporary Officer's Club.

By the end of World War I, the U.S. Navy had grown into a strong fleet, comparable to the British Navy. To make room for the newer warships in the fleet, many of the older warships were placed in reserve. Here we see several turn-of-the-century warships in reserve docked along Broad Street near the entrance of the Yard.

1919 was a time of growth on League Island. Building supplies are visible around Broad Street as new structures were being built for various purposes at the Navy Yard.

While growing with a number of new structures, the Yard was busy with naval work. Vessels were in for overhauls, repairs, and port calls. The Yard's various shops were at work producing the materials needed to keep the nation's fleet at sea.

This view looking northwest from the 350-ton crane shows that by 1921 the Yard was close to making complete use of League Island. However, within one year, the United States and other world powers would sign the Washington Naval Treaty which would limit the size of the world's navies.

The new buildings at PNSY were shops and factories which allowed the Yard to handle any type of repair a vessel might need. By 1921, the Shipyard was not the only resident of League Island. Aircraft were constructed at the Naval Aircraft Factory in the northeastern section of the facility near Mustin Naval Air Field.

In 1920, the Reserve Fleet Berthing area was established. At that time, ships berthed at Philadelphia consisted of "four-pipe" destroyers from World War I and auxiliary craft. The Reserve Fleet Berthing area is visible in the back area behind the factories. Because of its fresh water basin, Philadelphia was an ideal location to place warships.

The men at PNSY were responsible for maintaining the Yard as well as the ships. Here Yard workers are in the process of jacking Dry Dock # 3's east railroad crane back onto its tracks after running into an open switch on October 26, 1923.

This 1928 aerial view shows, from top to bottom, the Yard's docking Piers 1, 2, 3, 4, and 5 and also Dry Docks 1, 2, and 3.

The destroyers *Cassin* and *Shaw* are under construction on the shipways. Located between Dry Docks 3 and 4, the shipways were used for the construction of ships and could accommodate two small or one large warship.

This is the construction of the underwater ground ways for cruisers and light ships at Shipways #3, October 9, 1936. The ground ways provided a guide when ships were launched into the river after construction.

This is a caisson for Dry Dock #3 in Dry Dock #1 for overhaul and repair of its rubber gasket, July 7, 1941. The caisson was placed at the opening of a dry dock to allow the water to be pumped out after the vessel was in place.

Shot from the crane at Dry Dock #4, this photograph shows the Reserve Basin Bridge under construction on September 18, 1942. The bridge raises and lowers the center section to allow ships to enter and leave the Reserve Basin. Visible in the background on the right side is the Philadelphia Naval Hospital.

During World War II, the Naval Yard was also a training center. These carpenter's mates were being instructed in repair work and dry docking in order to prepare them to make emergency repair work at different advance bases.

Two of the *Iowa*-class battleships were built at Philadelphia during World War II. Here a "sleeved and yoked" gun barrel for USS *Wisconsin* (BB-64) is being placed aboard a barge on January 14, 1944.

Testing of engines and equipment was done at PNSY in its many shops. Here workers keep an eye on a model T-30 engine during testing.

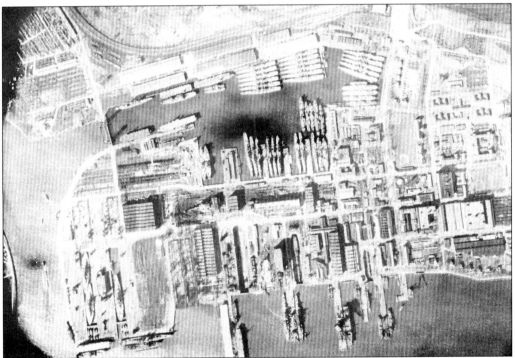

This is an aerial view of the Yard in 1952. With the end of World War II and the advances in naval technology, the United States Navy found itself with large numbers of obsolete vessels in good condition. Many of these ships were sent to Philadelphia for either overhauls or to be placed in reserve.

By the 1950s, the Philadelphia Reserve Fleet Berthing area had been renamed the Naval Inactive Ship Maintenance Facility, Philadelphia. The Inactive Ship facility was responsible for the mothballing and maintenance of vessels (like these cruisers) which were placed in reserve. In case of a national emergency, these ships could be reactivated, manned, and sent to bolster the strength of the fleet.

A shot of the Reserve Basin in 1971 shows many of the destroyers and cruisers assigned there.

Maintaining the fleet also meant maintaining the Yard. This progress photograph of Dry Dock #1 shows it half flooded as workers examine repair work.

Built of wood during the Spanish-American War, Dry Dock #1 was converted to concrete during the 1950s. Up close and drained, it is possible to see the size of Dry Dock #1, the smallest of the Yard's five dry docks.

Located near the Reserve Basin, Pier D was used in the repair of submarines. The building pictured served two functions. The upstairs were barracks for the crews of submarines that were in for repair or overhaul. The first floor was divided into shop areas for sheet metal, plumbing, and electrical work. The front of the building housed the shop stores, where supplies were kept. The building to the right was used for the repair of submarine batteries. The small sheds near the curb were the time clocks for Yard employees.

The marine railways were built for the repair of diesel electric submarines. It had the ability to move into the water under the submarine and then back into place, lifting the submarine out of the water for repair.

Quarters "C" were officer's quarters located near the riverfront. It was used to house Marine officers with the rank of major or colonel stationed at the base. Occasionally, they would be used for a Navy captain.

Quarters "M" were located near the river and are an example of the quarters assigned to the Shipyard commander and other high-ranking officers assigned to the Shipyard and Naval Base.

The Naval Shipyard was also used for various ceremonies. Here six chief petty officers have their picture taken aboard the USS *Croaker* (SS-246) after a retirement ceremony on September 17, 1962.

Building 100 was the Marine Barracks at the Philadelphia Naval Base. One of the original buildings and registered as a National Historic Landmark, the Barracks served as the enlisted men's living quarters and the administrative building for the Marines.

This shot from the 350-ton crane provides a view of Piers #5 and #6, as well as the Yard's shipways. Moored alongside are the USS *Berkeley* (DDG-15), USNS *Kings Port*, and USS *Long Beach* (CGN-9).

By 1963, PNSY was no longer isolated from the city of Philadelphia. Visible along the waterfront are two *Iowa*-class battleships. Besides constructing the *New Jersey* and the *Wisconsin*, the Yard provided a home for two of the dreadnoughts when mothballed.

The Main Gate on Broad Street was the primary access point to the Philadelphia Naval Shipyard. Constantly manned, here by Marine sentries and later by the Federal Police, this point was where all visitors had to pass to enter.

Building 6 was the administrative building for the Naval Base. Inside were administrative offices, a conference room, and the office of the base commander. The Philadelphia Naval Base was the headquarters for the Fourth Naval District. The building also housed a first-aid station in the area to the back right-hand side.

Near Dry Docks 4 and 5, this photograph shows the main Yard road running down League Island. In the center of the shot is one of the railroad cranes used around the dry docks for moving heavy equipment on and off ships.

USS *Guam* (LPH-9) is near completion in Dry Dock #5 in this 1965 photograph. Visible alongside of the dry dock are the railroad tracks used to move the cranes around during construction and repairs. The concrete slab to the right of the crane was later the site of a building constructed during the overhaul of the USS *Saratoga* to provide extra office and eating space for her crew.

This display from the 1968 Shipyard Commanders Conference, held at PNSY in the Officer's Club, shows the modernization of the Yard's steel-handling and storage area. It made use of area near the Reserve Basin and incorporated computers and advanced lifting equipment in the moving of steel plates from the storage area to the beginning of the processing area.

One of the most difficult jobs at the Yard was bringing a vessel into dry dock. It required precise handling and movement so that the ship would line up with the keel blocks as the water was pumped out of the dry dock. This photograph shows the USS *Conyngham* (DDG-17) being maneuvered into dry dock.

This is a photograph of the installation of the Melville statue on November 6, 1968. It was in honor of George W. Melville, the Navy's engineer-in-chief from 1887 to 1903. He played a prominent role in the development of U.S. Naval engineering at the turn of the century and also the growth of the American Navy.

The diving bell, the Trektite II, was used for ocean floor research sponsored by the government and private agencies. In between missions, it was stowed at the Yard near Building #20.

A submarine diesel engine is shown here in storage in Building 592. PNSY had the capabilities to overhaul and rebuild any part of a vessel.

Building 1070 can be seen in this photograph under construction in 1972. It was built as the new electronics building and is attached to Building 546, which was used for hydraulics testing and the construction of PT boats. The structure in the foreground housed shop stores, the rigger's loft, and a cafeteria.

Building 11 was the Shipyard's Administrative Building, housing the production office, the administrative offices, and the shipyard commander's office. Located on the east side of First Street between Philip and Porter Avenues, it was completed in 1903 at a cost of $133,400.

The area in this photograph is directly across Broad Street from Building 6. The quarter circle structure in the foreground is Building 63, originally the round house for the railroad that brought supplies and materials to the various Yard shops. The building was later used as an automotive repair facility by 07 Shop, Yard Transportation. It was torn down in 1978. The one-story structure to the left was used to house paint lockers and the safety office. To the left of that is the back of the Shipyard's firehouse.

PNSY workers align the steam catapult aboard a U.S. aircraft carrier undergoing a Service Life Extension Program (SLEP) overhaul during the 1980s. This program kept the Yard open into the early 1990s.

A catapult test is taking place aboard the USS *Kitty Hawk* during her SLEP overhaul on October 26, 1990. A 50-ton dead load called "Big Bertha" was fired into the Delaware River as part of the test.

This crossover connects Buildings 11 and 7. Building 11 housed administrative and officers' offices, and Building 7 contained offices for design, engineering, and planning.

This is the exterior view of Building 546, a hydraulics building.

Building 20, the Foundry, is where ship propellers were molded and finished, as well as smaller castings of various parts. The raised box on the side of the building stores sand used in the sand-blasting process. The Foundry is one of the few building that remained in operation after the Yard closed.

These perpendicular buildings are Buildings 47 and 16. Located across the street from Building 20, Building 47 (on the left) was used for propeller dressing and balancing, and Building 16 (on the right) housed a machine shop.

Two

The Ships

This is a photograph of the USS *Relief* (AH-1) just before launching on December 23, 1919. She was the sixth ship of the U.S. Navy to carry the name and the first designed and built from the keel up as a hospital ship. She served in World War II, receiving five battle stars, evacuating nearly ten thousand fighting men from scenes of combat in almost every military campaign of the Pacific Theater, and steaming the equivalent of nearly four times around the world.

This is the launching of the USS *Minneapolis* (CA-36) on September 6, 1933. Serving in the Pacific, she was at sea for gunnery practice when the Japanese attacked Pearl Harbor. Afterwards, she was on patrol until January 1942, when she joined the raid of the Gilberts and Marshalls. *Minneapolis* saw action at the Battle of Coral Sea and at Midway. She fired the first shot at the Battle of Tassafaronga, where she was badly damaged, but was saved by her own crew. She was back in the Pacific by August 1943 for twenty months of front line duty, which included every major Pacific operation except Iwo Jima. For service in World War II, the *Minneapolis* received sixteen battle stars.

USS *Cassin* and *Shaw* are being launched in this photograph taken on October 28, 1935. *Shaw* (DD-373), on the right, served in the Atlantic and Pacific before World War II. She was dry docked for repairs at Pearl Harbor when the Japanese attacked. Severely damaged, she was sent to San Francisco for repairs, returning to Pearl Harbor on August 31, 1942. *Shaw*'s war service included escort duty in connection with many key campaigns in the Pacific Theater; this service earned her eleven battle stars.

USS *Cassin* (DD-372) is shown leaving the Philadelphia Naval Shipyard. Prior to World War II, she served in the Pacific area as part of the Hawaiian Detachment. She was in dry dock on December 7, 1941 along with the USS *Downes* (DD-375) and *Pennsylvania* (BB-38). Damaged in the Japanese raid and considered lost, outstanding salvage efforts saved her. *Cassin* went on to serve in many of the key campaigns of the Pacific Theater and received six battle stars.

USS *Wichita* (CA-45) is moving down the ways in this November, 16, 1937 photograph. She served in the Atlantic, leading neutrality patrols in the Caribbean and showing the flag in South American ports. With U.S. entry into World War II, *Wichita* saw action in both the Atlantic and Pacific Theaters, earning her thirteen battle stars.

PNSY didn't just build vessels for the U.S. Navy. In this picture, the Coast Guard cutters *Campbell*, *Ingham*, *Duane*, and *Taney* are in the final stages of construction in Dry Dock #4.

The four cutters are dressed up in preparation of their christening.

The Coast Guard follows the traditions of the sea, as a crowd gathers for the christening of the four cutters. Here, the christening of U.S.C.G. cutter *George W. Campbell* takes place.

USS *Washington* (BB-56) is riding the ways on June 1, 1940. She was the eighth ship to carry the name and the first battleship built at PNSY. She went from her shakedown and training cruise straight into World War II, where she served in the Atlantic as flagship of Battleship Division 6 and later of Task Force 39. On August 23, 1942, she transferred to the Pacific Theater, where she served for the rest of the war. Her World War II service earned her thirteen battle stars and carried her from the Arctic Circle to the western Pacific.

USS *Antietam* (CV-36) is shown here under way in the Pacific. Launched from Philadelphia Naval Shipyard on August 20, 1944, along with the USS *Chicago* and USS *Los Angeles*, she reached the Pacific too late to participate in World War II. She was placed in reserve on June 12, 1949, but returned to service two years later because of the Korean conflict, where she earned two battle stars. After being modernized in 1952, she served in the Atlantic Fleet until 1957.

This vessel, the third to carry the name *Chicago* (CA-136), was launched from the Philadelphia Naval Shipyard on August 20, 1944 and immediately proceeded to the Pacific where she participated in various operations. After the war, the *Chicago* made several patrols in the Pacific. On November 1, 1958, work began to convert the ship from a gun cruiser to a guided-missile cruiser.

This is a photograph of the laying of the keels of the USS *Butler* (DD-636) and USS *Gheradi* (DD-37) on September 16, 1941. Launched on February 12, 1942, these two destroyers saw action in both the Atlantic and Pacific Theaters. *Gheradi* provided fire support for invasion forces on D-Day and received five battle stars during the war. *Butler* received the Navy Unit Commendation for her service at Okinawa and also four battle stars.

In this September 14, 1943 photograph, the laying of the keel for the USS *Princeton* (CV-37) is shown. Originally laid down as the *Valley Forge*, she was renamed after the previous USS *Princeton* was lost in August 1943 in the Pacific. She saw action in Korea, where she earned eight battle stars, and off the coast of Viet Nam. *Princeton* was designated the recovery ship for Apollo 10 in April 1969.

USS *Philadelphia* (CL-41) was built at the Naval Shipyard between May 1935 and November 1936 and also served in the Atlantic Theater during World War II, providing both escort and fire support. She was transferred to the Brazilian Navy in 1947 and was renamed the *Cruzador Barroso* (C11).

Built across the river at the New York Shipbuilding Association in Camden, New Jersey, the *Savannah* (CL-42) came to the Philadelphia Naval Shipyard for alterations and repairs during her service life. After service in World War II, she was sent to the Philadelphia Naval Shipyard as part of the Inactive Fleet.

This is the crest of the Philadelphia Naval Shipyard, the Mainstay of the Fleet. In front of the Yard's trademark 350-ton Hammerhead crane are the silhouettes of a surface ship and a submarine, the focus of work in Philadelphia.

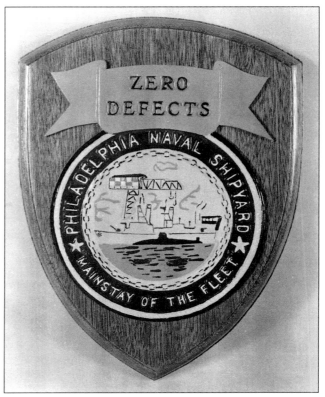

The USS *Cabot* (CVL-28) is being removed from the dry dock after the painting of the bottom in preparation for being reactivated. Having been placed out of commission in reserve at Philadelphia on February 11, 1947, the ship was being reactivated to serve as a training carrier near Pensacola, Florida.

This is the river run of the USS *Guarina* (AGSS-362) on July 21, 1954, after an extensive overhaul. The raised platform over the aft torpedo room was used in the refueling of seaplanes at sea and was dubbed the "flight deck."

USS *Washoe County* (LST-1165), a tank landing ship, is in dry dock at PNSY for repairs in 1955. In 1958, the *Washoe County* transferred from the Atlantic to the Pacific fleet, In the Pacific, she would participate in transporting Marines and their equipment to Viet Nam, where she earned twelve battle stars.

USS *William T. Powell* (DE-213) is shown in dry dock for repairs. The *Powell* saw service in World War II and was later home-ported at PNSY on November 5, 1948, as a Naval Reserve Training (NRT) ship.

USS *Wisconsin* (BB-64) is shown under way in 1955. She was one of two *Iowa*-class battleship built at PNSY during World War II, seeing action in the Pacific. After the war, *Wisconsin* was used for reserve training cruises and was placed in mothball on July 1, 1948. She was reactivated during the Korean War, where once again she saw service. In 1958, the battleship was again deactivated and sent to PNSY until the Naval build-up during the Reagan administration called her back to service. *Wisconsin* saw more recent action during Desert Storm. She returned to Philadelphia again to be deactivated as the Navy downsized in the 1990s.

Many of the warships that saw service in World War II were placed in reserve and sent to Philadelphia in the 1950s to be mothballed. This stern view is of USS *Chester* (CA-27). Launched at New York Shipbuilding Co. in Camden, New Jersey, on July 3, 1929, the *Chester* served in the Atlantic and later in the Pacific, where she saw action during World War II. *Chester* earned eleven battle stars for World War II action. She came to PNSY on January 30, 1946, where she was deactivated and placed in reserve.

Also built across the river in Camden, New Jersey, the USS *Montpelier* (CL-57), moored along Broad Street, was launched on February 12, 1942. Her war service took her to the Pacific Theater, where she provided fire support for amphibious landings. After the war, she was sent to PNSY for deactivation and placed in reserve on January 24, 1947. She had thirteen battle stars.

USS *Houston* (CL-81) is seen here in the Reserve Basin in 1959 prior to being scrapped. The cruiser, launched in 1943, saw action in the Pacific Theater, participating in the invasion of the Marianas Islands and the Battle of the Philippine Sea. She was severely damaged in preparation for the invasion of Okinawa but was saved. After the war, she conducted training and goodwill cruises in the Atlantic until coming to PNSY in August 1947, where she was decommissioned on December 15, 1947.

Originally launched in 1943 as a light gun cruiser, the USS *Little Rock* began a conversion to a guided-missile cruiser on May 23, 1957. Here she is being recommissioned in Philadelphia on June 3, 1960.

Recommissioning of the USS *Burrfish* on January 17, 1961, was in response to the need to bolster the nation's submarine force to counter the Soviet threat, which brought many World War II boats out of reserve and back into the fleet.

This is an aerial view of the USS *Long Beach* (CGN-9), the first nuclear-powered warship in history. She arrived at PNSY on April 28, 1962, for an extended overhaul, which included modifications and improvements to her electronics and radar components.

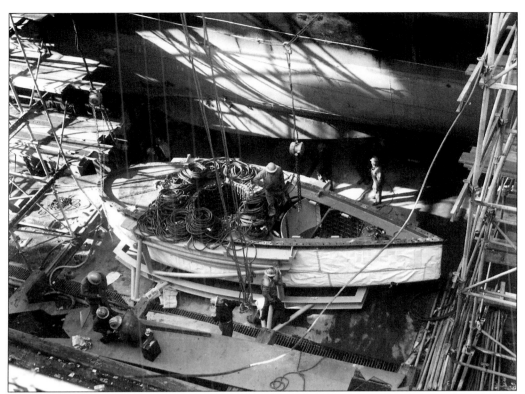

PNSY workers prepare to install an AN/SQS sonar dome and transducer to the USS *Noa* (DD-841) as part of the Fleet Rehabilitation and Modernization (FRAM) 1 overhaul program, which upgraded the anti-submarine capability of older warships.

The Soviet submarine threat required destroyers to be upgraded to protect fleet assets. Here the USS *Noa* is seen in dry dock after the addition of her new sonar dome. Among her service credits, *Noa* was the vessel that recovered John Glenn and his space capsule on February 19, 1962, after America put its first astronaut into space.

One of the various projects done at PNSY during the 1960s was the conversion of submarines to radar picket boats; this alteration required that the boat be cut in half and then stretched. Here the bow of a submarine is visible with the stretching equipment in the foreground.

After stretching, a section was placed in the submarine to accommodate the new radar equipment. In this photograph, a section is being prepared to be lowered into a submarine.

This photograph shows the arrival of the midget submarine *X-1* at PNSY on April 23, 1962. The Yard conducted research and made alterations to vessels for various Navy projects.

PTF-1 and *PTF-2* are shown at Pier 5, where modifications were made to these PT boats in Building 547 for tests to learn if they could be quieted for covert river operations.

USS *Bang* (SS-385) makes a test run on the Delaware River after an overhaul at PNSY.

USS *Halfbeak* (SS-352) rests alongside Pier D at PNSY. She was in for an overhaul and the addition of new radar equipment.

USS *Hake* (AGSS-256) is pictured alongside the wharf. She had been assigned to PNSY as a reserve training ship for the Fourth Naval District.

Various service craft were assigned to PNSY as floating workshops and storage areas. These craft were also maintained at the Yard. Here we see PNSY service craft in Dry Dock #4 for overhaul.

Yard tugs were important to operations at PNSY. YTM-359 *Pawtucket* was one of the many tugs used at the Yard to move vessels to their proper location.

The *Ethiopian Victory* is entering dry dock for a $7.5 million overhaul to convert her to a fleet ballistic missile resupply vessel as part of the nation's new ballistic missile submarine program.

USS *Corporal* (SS-346) makes a river run in this 1965 photograph after Yard work at PNSY. She was sold in 1973 to Turkey, where she was renamed the *Ikinci Inonu*.

This is a keel laying ceremony for LPH-11, USS *New Orleans*, March 1, 1966, at PNSY. The *New Orleans* was one of four *Iwo Jima*-class amphibious assault ships built in Philadelphia. These vessels were the first ships built specifically to operate helicopters.

After an overhaul at PNSY, the USS *Cutlass* (SS-478) is shown here on a test run on the Delaware. Originally launched in 1944, the *Cutlass* entered her patrol area in the Pacific one day after the Japanese surrendered. After the war, the *Cutlass* patrolled in the Atlantic Ocean, visiting PNSY on three occasions for overhaul and modernization.

This is the lead ship of the *Newport*-class of tank-landing ships under construction at PNSY in 1967, two month after the keel was laid. These amphibious ships were designed to be "beached" and sustain a speed of 20 knots.

The only battleship reactivated for service in Viet Nam, the USS *New Jersey* (BB-62), is being moved from the Reserve Basin to a pier at PNSY in preparation of her rejoining the fleet.

Seen here off the coast of Oahu, Hawaii, in 1967, the USS *Newport News* (CA-148) was the world's last active heavy cruiser. She saw extensive action in Viet Nam as a fire support platform. She was decommissioned in 1975 and sent to PNSY as part of the Reserve Fleet.

USS *Manitowac* (LST-1180), under construction at PNSY, was the second of the *Newport*-class amphibious ships built at the Yard.

Another one of the Yard's tugs, YTM-149, is seen in front of Pier 4 with the 350-ton Hammerhead crane.

Yard tug YTM-761 *Menasha* maneuvers USS *Fort Mandan* (LSD-21) into position alongside Pier 4. The *Menasha* was part of a class of tugs built to an experimental design with cycloidal propellers that provide a high degree of maneuverability and enable them to turn 360 degrees within their length.

The USS *Sumter* (LST-1181) is shown under way during trials on the Delaware Bay in July 1970. She was the last ship of this class to be built at PNSY.

This is a shot of the USS *Bonefish* (SS-582) in dry dock at PNSY. One of the *Barbell*-class submarines, these were the last diesel-electric combat submarines built in the United States and the last to be used in U.S. Navy service. They were also the first to incorporate the "tear-drop" high-speed hull design.

USS *Albany* (CG-10) arrives here at PNSY on July 6, 1973, to begin a complex overhaul, which was scheduled to take place in two parts and last ten months. When commissioned in 1943, the *Albany* was originally a gun cruiser (CA-123). She was converted to a missile cruiser in November 1957.

USS *Belknap* (CG-26) is pictured here under way. She arrived at PNSY on January 30, 1976, to be rebuilt after colliding with the USS *John F. Kennedy* (CV-67) in the Ionian Sea on the night of November 22, 1975. She returned to sea in April 1980. Today, the *Belknap* is part of the reserve fleet at PNSY.

The USS *Barry* (DD-933) also is pictured under way. She came to Philadelphia on August 22, 1982, for a port visit after leaving New York City. PNSY was the host for any Naval vessel that came to the city for a port visit.

The USS *Clifton Sprague* (FFG-16) arrives at PNSY to become part of the reserve force in 1984 (three years after being commissioned). The Navy transferred new frigates to the Naval Reserve Force in an effort to modernize it.

USS *Coral Sea* (CV-43) is pictured at Pier 4 at PNSY. Originally launched in 1946, the *Coral Sea* landed more aircraft than any other carrier, recording her 300,000th aircraft recovery on December 24, 1981.

USS *Saratoga* (CV-60) undergoes a SLEP overhaul in Dry Dock #5 at PNSY. The first carrier to undergo the $550 million overhaul to add fifteen years to her service life, the *Saratoga* arrived at the Yard on September 30, 1980, and left in February 1983.

The USS *Forrestal* (CV-59), the U.S. Navy's first super-carrier, was the second carrier to undergo the SLEP overhaul. In 1992, the *Forrestal* returned to PNSY for conversion to a training carrier, until it was decided to decommission her on September 11, 1993. She is currently moored at Pier 4 at PNSY alongside the *Saratoga*.

USS *Guadalcanal* (LPH 7) is pictured being moved to a pier at PNSY. Built at Philadelphia, she was launched on March 16, 1963, and served in the Atlantic. She was decommissioned and sent to Philadelphia in 1995.

Two destroyers are in dry dock for overhaul. Notice the shack constructed over the aft area of the destroyer in the foreground. Such structures were used to cover work areas for environmental and security reasons.

Before becoming the Air-Sea-Space Museum in New York City, the USS *Intrepid* (CV-11) was docked in the Reserve Basin at PNSY. She came to the Reserve Basin in 1976 after being decommissioned at the Yard on March 15, 1974. The *Intrepid* saw service in World War II and Viet Nam. She also was the recovery ship for Scott Carpenter's *Aurora 7* space capsule in 1962 and for John Young and Virgil Grissom's *Molly Brown* space capsule in 1965. Here the *Intrepid* is being towed out of the Reserve Basin on her way to New York in 1982.

Another ship memorial to come from PNSY's Reserve Basin was the USS *Kidd* (DD-661). The *Kidd* was turned over to the State of Louisiana on April 2, 1982, to become a memorial in Baton Rouge. She saw action in World War II and Korea, where she earned four battle stars in each conflict. She arrived at Philadelphia on January 25, 1960, to conduct Naval Reserve Training cruises until she was decommissioned on June 19, 1964.

USS *Constellation* (CV-64) arrives at Pier 4 in preparation for her SLEP overhaul. By the 1990s, the SLEP program was the main factor keeping the Yard open.

Three

PNSY and the Community

Civilian employees were the backbone of PNSY. Although a military installation, non-military personnel were the foremen, engineers, and the ones who built and repaired the ships. Here, the men from the Electrical Shop Inside-Outside Service Maintenance sit for a group photograph in 1930.

The year 1951 marked the 150th anniversary of PNSY. The occasion was celebrated by special events, including the crowning of a Miss Philadelphia Naval Shipyard winner and a parade through the city.

Yard employees were very active in supporting the community and the Yard. During World War II, they participated actively in war bond drives, and afterwards, they took part in community and Navy events. One such event was the Navy Red Cross blood drive.

The Philadelphia Naval Shipyard Apprentice School taught men the skills they needed to work at the Yard. The school was a constant source of manpower and education at the Yard. This is the June 1951 graduating class.

Many of the Naval Shipyard's employees lived in New Jersey. Rather than driving across the Walt Whitman Bridge and parking on the base, many of these workers chose to come to work on the ferry, the *Reliance*, that ran between National Park, New Jersey, and the Shipyard.

A main means of interaction between the Yard and the community was the Armed Forces Day open house. One weekend in May, PNSY would open its gates and invite the public and the families of employees onto the base to let them see both what the Navy and the Shipyard in Philadelphia did. This tool display is from 06 Shop, which was housed in Building 634 near Pier 6.

Protective gear was very important in day-to-day operations at the Yard. This display gives a sampling of the various equipment used by 06 Shop.

Part of an open house visit included visiting ships that were at the Yard for repair or part of the reserve fleet. The *Siboney* (CVE-112) was part of the reserve fleet at Philadelphia, arriving at the Yard on July 31, 1956. The vessels at PNSY gave visitors a taste of the various types of ships in the fleet.

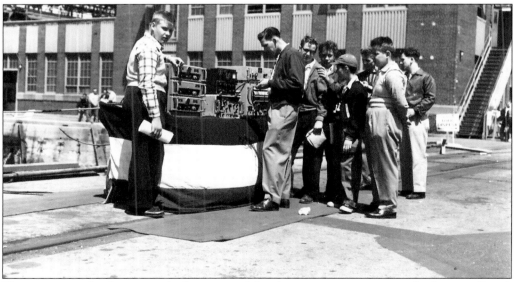

These visitors take the time to look at some of the electronics equipment on display near Pier 6, Building 574. Building 574 was a workshop, with offices located upstairs and shop stores and workshop located downstairs.

The Armed Forces Day open house allowed the various Yard activities to present displays of their work and equipment.

The Philadelphia Naval Shipyard String Band was an unofficial organization made up of Yard workers who volunteered to be part of the band. It was organized in 1946 by the Employee Services Division of the Industrial Relations Department. The group performed at nearly all Naval Base functions and helped create a family-type of atmosphere.

Building 541 was a big catch-all structure used as a prefabrication building during the World War II period, when constructions were done at the Yard. The right side of the photograph shows a partition wall, while the left side shows the outer wall.

This portable generator was operated by 38 Shop, outside mechanist. This display is located inside Building 546.

This is the Apprentice Graduating Class of 1961–1962.

The Armed Forces Day's open house was also a time for fun. The parade ground in front of the Marine Barracks was set up with carnival rides.

The Marines took part in the open house by demonstrating some of the equipment and weapons used in the field.

Located on the eighth floor in Building 5, this computer control room housed the ATM machine, which regulated the numerical control machinery for drilling and used punch cards.

This Sikorsky S-58 on display at the open house provided another dimension for visitors as they learned more about the Navy. During the early part of the century, the Yard also housed the Naval Aircraft Factory and Mustin Field, which were a part of the birth of Naval aviation.

Inside Building 20, which is the Foundry, is 23 Shop, the forge. The area shown here was used for casting small work, such as fittings.

This display in the south end of Building 543 shows the work of 56 Shop (pipe-fitters) and 57 Shop (insulators). The pre-form insulation covers on display were fabricated upstairs. The area behind the display were the shop offices.

This is a close-up view of display in Building 543.

The open house was also an opportunity to learn about the equipment used by the fleet. Here a crewman tells visitors about the missile launcher on board the USS *Strauss*.

Occasionally, an open house featured more than U.S. Naval vessels for visitors to tour. In 1963, the Spanish training ship *Juan Sebastian De Elcano* was in Philadelphia for a port visit.

Visitors learn about the work done by 17 Shop in Building 25. 17 Shop was responsible for duct work on ships and the ventilation systems.

Inside the submarine repair shop on Pier D, visitors look at a display of various coolers used on board a submarine.

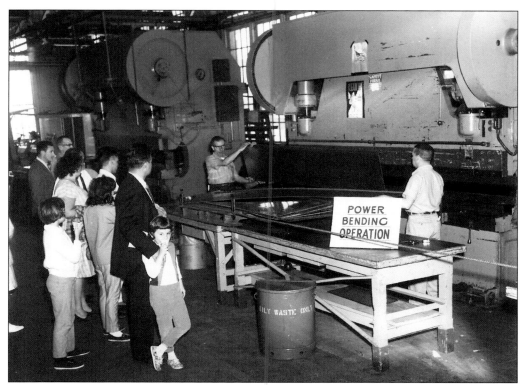

The power-bending operation demonstration was done by 17 Shop, inside of Building 25 where they did lightweight sheet-metal work.

One of the vessels moored at PNSY, the USS *Roman* (DD-782) was open for ship tours. At the Yard, visitors were able to look at almost every type of U.S. warship, from a submarine to a battleship.

Inside of Building 47, workers demonstrate the means for balancing a propeller at PNSY. This building was across the street from the Foundry. After the Foundry, propellers were brought to Building 47 to allow final refinements before being sent to a ship.

Located in the middle of Building 543, the machines on the left were used for bending hollow pipe. Because of the stress and difficulty of this procedure, work on these machines was rotated among Yard employees.

Moored alongside Pier 4, USS *Wisconsin* (BB-64), the last dreadnought built in the United States, was opened for tours during Armed Forces weekend. The *Wisconsin* was placed in reserve at the Philadelphia Naval Shipyard after the Korean War.

In contrast to the spacious size of the of the *Wisconsin*, tours were given of the cramped accommodations aboard the diesel submarine USS *Skate* (SS-256). Behind the *Skate* is the slip where the ferry from National Park, New Jersey, docked.

A sign of the school's endurance, the graduating Class of 1971 from the Philadelphia Naval Shipyard Apprentice School have their picture taken in front of Building 11.

The Philadelphia Naval Shipyard Fire Department built this float for use in parades during the 1974 holiday season. The Yard's fire department was active in the community both on and off the base through various events.

The ferry *Polaris* brought employees to work from across the river. The *Polaris* replaced the *Reliance* and was used until the Yard closed.

Arriving from New Jersey by ferry, these Yard employees were greeted in the morning by a Marine guard to check security identification.

Four

PNSY and the World

During World War II, PNSY performed repair work on damaged Allied warships. On the left is the British warship HMS *Argonaut*. She arrived on April 30, 1943, for repairs of damage she received. She returned to action on November 12th that same year.

A sign of PNSY's commitment to strengthening the friendship with U.S. allies, this wall is adorned with the ship's crest of the foreign vessels that past through the Yard, as yet another is being placed on it.

The Turkish submarine *Canakkale* on a river run after the completion of an overhaul at PNSY in 1955. The boat was originally the USS *Bumper* before being turned over by the United States to Turkey. During the Cold War, the United States leased and sold many of its World War II destroyers, submarines, and cruisers to Allied nations to help build up their naval strength.

RADM. SUMIO MATSUZAKI, HEAD OF THE TECHNICAL DIVISION
OF THE JAPANESE MARITIME STAFF OFFICE WITH CAPT.
KENZO KAWAKITA AND CAPT. JUNJI UOSUMI.
PHILA. NAVAL SHIPYARD   5 DEC 1955

Ten years after the war, the head of the Technical Division of the Japanese Maritime Staff Office, Rear Admiral Sumio Matsuzaki, along with Captains Kenzo Kawakita and Junji Uosumi, came to PNSY for a tour of the Yard and the various methods employed there.

One of the traditions at the Yard was for visiting foreign officers to sign the Commander's Visitor Log. Here an admiral from Turkey signs the log.

The Navy is very rich in traditions and ceremonies. One such special ceremony took place when a ship was turned over to another country. Here, the crew of the Spanish destroyer *Almiante Valdez*, formerly the USS *Converse* (DD-569), wait to man their new ship.

Visiting naval officers from Canada pose for a picture with the Shipyard commander during a visit in 1961.

Many of the submarines overhauled for foreign nations at PNSY were former U.S. Navy warships. The Turkish submarine *Gur*, formerly the USS *Chub* (SS-329), is in for an overhaul in the Marine Railways.

The *Custodio De Mello* (U-26) from Brazil arrived at PNSY on June 14, 1966. Built in Japan as a transport, she was turned into a training vessel in July 1961.

This aerial view shows the Venezuelan submarine *Carite* (S-11) in the Delaware Bay in 1966.

Visiting in July 1967, these German frigates are the *Braunschweig* (F225), the *Augsburg* (F222), and the *Lubeck* (F224). These ships were 2,400 tons, 110 meters long, and could make 30 knots. Underneath the covering on the bow is the forward gun emplacement.

USS *Jack* is pictured alongside a pier on January 24, 1957, in preparation for her transfer to Greece. She had served in the Pacific during World War II, where she earned the Presidential Unit Citation and seven battle stars. She was loaned to the Royal Hellenic Navy on April 21, 1958, where she became the HHMS *Amfitriti* (S-09).

Following service in the U.S. Navy after reactivation in 1948, the USS *Cabot* (AVT-3) was turned over to Spain in 1967. In Spain, she became the SNS *De Dalo* (PH-1) and served into the late 1980s.

This display at the Shipyard Commanders Conference held at PNSY in the 'O' Club on October 15, 1968, shows the assistance the Yard provided to foreign nations.

This is the fiscal 1970 Naval Shipyard Management Training course for senior foreign naval officers. Present are officers from Pakistan, Turkey, Korea, Italy, Indonesia, Brazil, Mexico, China, Chile, Greece, and Vietnam. These and other officers came to PNSY to learn the skills to run a shipyard. When officers from rival fleets were present, it could lead to competition among them to make sure that they learned everything the others did. This also placed a burden on instructors not to act in a manner that could be interpreted as favoritism.

In for a port visit in June 1971 is the HMS *Cleopatra*.

Imperial Iranian ships *Palang* and *Babr* are shown here in dry dock. Purchased in March 1971, they were delivered in October 1973 after major refits at PNSY, which included installation of more powerful air-conditioning, a telescoping helicopter hangar, and modifications to the armament. The ships are still in use by the Iranian navy.

Photographed on the Delaware River on July 5, 1972, while at PNSY for overhaul, the USS *Clamagrove* (SS-343) was sold to Turkey in 1975.

Workers conduct a flooding drill aboard the Greek submarine *Papannikolis* (SS-114) alongside Pier D. Formerly the USS *Hardhead* (SS-365), she was purchased by Greece on July 26, 1972.

This is the HMS *Devonshire* at PNSY after her arrival on June 20, 1973, for a port visit.

The German destroyer *Lutjen* (D-185) arrives in Philadelphia on July 18, 1973, for an upgrade in systems. Since her design was based on the USS *Charles F. Adams*-class destroyer, PNSY was a natural choice to handle the work.

The Brazilian submarine *Ceara* (S14) is departing the Reserve Basin at PNSY in September 1974. Formerly the USS *Amberjack*, the boat had been sold to Brazil in October 1973 and had come to PNSY for a four month RAV in 1974.

Two Israeli missile boats are moored at Pier 1 during a port visit in July 1976. The first boat is the *Yaffo*. Pier 1 was the customary location where visiting foreign vessels were docked.

Queen Elizabeth arrived in Philadelphia on July 23, 1976, on the Royal Yacht *Britannia* during an East Coast trip from England. Her yacht docked at PNSY, where she was given the proper honors of a visiting dignitary.

HMCS *Nipigon* (DDH-266) from Canada visited Philadelphia for a port call on June 4, 1986, as part of Philadelphia's Century IV celebration. As was custom, the Yard played host to the vessel and handled all press information.

The French helicopter carrier FNS *Jeanne D'Arc* docked at Pier 2 in 1984.

HMS *Penelope* (F127) is docking at PNSY with help of the Yard tug *Mascoutah*.